Q&A Kids

PLANTS

AMY CHAPMAN ANGELIKA SCUDAMORE

WINDMILL BOOKS

Published in 2026 by Windmill Books,
an Imprint of Rosen Publishing
2544 Clinton St.
Buffalo, NY 14224

First published in Great Britain in 2026
by Wayland

Editor: Sarah Peutrill
Designer: Lisa Peacock

Some of the text in this book was
first published in Fact Cat: Plants
by Izzi Howell

Cataloging-in-Publication Data

Names: Chapman, Amy, author. | Scudamore, Angelika, illustrator.
Title: Plants / Amy Chapman, illustrated by Angelika Scudamore.
Description: Buffalo, NY : Windmill Books, 2026. | Series: Q & A kids | Includes glossary and index.
Identifiers: ISBN 9781725396319 (pbk.) | ISBN 9781725396326 (library bound) | ISBN 9781725396333 (ebook)
Subjects: LCSH: Botany--Juvenile literature. | Plants--Juvenile literature.
Classification: LCC QK49.C437 2026 | DDC 580--dc23

Printed in the United States of America

CPSIA Compliance Information: Batch #CSWM26
For Further Information contact Rosen Publishing
at 1-800-237-9932

CONTENTS

Can you spot me in this book? There are 16 to find, not counting this one.

WHAT ARE PLANTS?

Q. What are plants?

A. Plants are living things. Like animals and humans, they need food and water. They grow taller and bigger and reproduce to make new plants.

Plants come in many sizes, from tall trees to tiny green algae. Some types of algae are so small that they can only be seen through a microscope!

THINK ABOUT IT
Have you got any favorite plants?

From tiny algae (through a microscope) to THIS!!

PLANT HABITATS

Q. Where do plants grow?

A. Plants grow in many habitats around the world. Plants are often different from one habitat to another.

MATCH IT

Can you match the descriptions A–D to the correct pictures 1–4?

1.

2.

3.

A. Spiky cactuses grow in dry deserts.

4.

B. Plants that don't need much light, such as ferns, grow on the shady woodland floor.

C. There are many types of brightly colored flowers in the rainforest.

D. Slimy seaweed is found in seas and oceans.

PARTS OF A PLANT

Q. Are all plants the same?

A. They can look very different, but most have similar parts.

Most plants have three main parts – the roots, the stem, and the leaves. Each part of the plant has a different job. Plant roots grow underground in the soil. The stem and the leaves grow above ground.

Plant roots take in water and nutrients from the soil. This water travels up the plant stem to the leaves. Plant roots are very strong. Some can even break through stone and concrete! The job of the leaves is to make food for the plant (see page 20).

THINK ABOUT IT

Can you work out what the missing labels are for the plant?

C.
B.
A.

PLANT LIFE CYCLES

Q. How long do plants live for?

A. The life cycle of a plant can last a few months or hundreds of years. This drawing shows the life cycle of a dandelion, which is a flowering plant.

The life cycle of a dandelion can last for several years. It will release seeds several times before it dies. However, some plants, such as sunflowers, only release seeds once before they die.

THINK ABOUT IT

The life cycles of most flowering plants follow the seasons. In spring, they grow from seeds. Their flowers bloom in summer and their seeds develop in autumn. What happens to most seeds in the winter?

5. The plant releases its seeds (see page 18).

3. The stem and leaves grow.

4. The flowers on the adult plant make seeds (see page 12).

SEEDS

Q. Do all plants grow from seeds?

A. Most plants grow from seeds. When a seed is in a dark, warm, damp place, its hard shell breaks open and it sprouts roots and a shoot.

This is how a bean plant grows from a seed.

1. Roots grow down into the soil.

2. Shoot grows up and out of the soil.

3. Leaves grow on the stem.

THINK ABOUT IT

Ellie is growing a bean seed in a pot. What does the seed need to grow? Look at the picture for clues.

BULBS

Q. What do plants grow from if not from seeds?

A. Plants such as daffodils and tulips grow from a type of round root, called a bulb. Bulbs are filled with food, which the plant uses to grow new leaves.

Onions and garlic are the bulbs of plants that we can eat.

THINK ABOUT IT

Bulbs are usually planted in autumn or winter. In which season will their roots and shoots grow?

FLOWERS

Q. Why are flowers such bright colors?

A. Flowers often have a strong smell or brightly colored petals to attract insects. Some are filled with nectar, a sweet liquid that insects like to drink.

Flowers have petals around the outside and a powder called pollen in the center. Most flowers need pollen from other plants to make seeds. Insects such as bees carry pollen from one flower to another. The bee picks up pollen on its legs when it lands on a flower to drink nectar. It then carries this pollen to the next plant. Pollen is also carried by other animals and the wind.

CHALLENGE

Follow the path to find out which types of flower are pollinated by insects like these bees, and which type is wind pollinated.

Apple
Lotus
Dandelion

FRUITS AND SEED PODS

Q. What happens when the flower is pollinated?

A. Once a flower has been pollinated, its petals drop off. A fruit or a seed pod, filled with seeds, grows in its place.

Seeds are scattered by the wind and by animals. If all of a plant's seeds grew next to each other, there wouldn't be enough space, light, or water for them to survive.

Coconuts, the seeds of the palm tree, are spread by water. Palm trees often grow on beaches and so coconuts fall into the sea. They are carried to different beaches where new palm trees grow.

When animals eat fruits or seed pods, the plant seeds pass through their bodies and come out in their droppings.

THINK ABOUT IT

What is another way that animals can spread seeds?

MAKING FOOD

Q. Do plants eat food like we do?

A. No, but they do need food. Plants are very clever – they can make food themselves, using water, energy from the Sun, and a gas called carbon dioxide.

This happens in the leaves of the plant. The process of plants making their own food is called photosynthesis (say *fo-toe-sin-thuh-sis*).

Plants die without sunlight and water because they are not able to make food. If you have plants in your house, it's important to water them and keep them in a sunny place. Plants make a gas called oxygen during photosynthesis. People and other animals need to breathe oxygen to survive.

FIND IT

Which of these plants has not had enough sunlight and water? How can you tell?

PLANTS AND ANIMALS

Q. Can animals make their own food like plants?

A. No they can't, so plants are an important source of food for many animals. Animals that only eat plants are called herbivores.

Omnivore animals, such as bears, eat plants and other animals. Goats are herbivores. A goat will eat almost any plant, even stinging nettles.

Most herbivores eat a range of different plants, but some herbivores only eat one or two types of plant. The giant panda only eats bamboo stems and koalas mainly eat the leaves of the eucalyptus tree! Giraffes like small spiky acacia leaves.

MATCH IT

Match the animals to the type of plant they like to eat.

1.

2.

3.

4.

A.

B.

C.

D.

PLANTS AND PEOPLE

Q. Do plants all taste the same?

A. No! For instance, peas, carrots, and broccoli all come from plants and they all taste quite different.

Farmers grow most of the plants that humans eat. They plant orchards of fruit trees and large fields of crops, such as wheat and corn.

Roots

Seeds

MATCH IT

Humans can only eat certain parts of some plants. Which part of these plants A–F do we eat?

Leaves

Fruit

A. Carrots

B. Lettuce

C. Peas

D. Apples

E. Leek

F. Cauliflower

USEFUL PLANTS

Q. What else are plants useful for?

A. Many things! People have always made use of plants. Any part of a plant can be useful: the roots, stems, flowers, fruits, or seeds. For example the leaves of the palm tree can be woven together to make walls and roofs. Its coconut fruit can be made into oils for soap and fuel. Plants can also clothe us, give us medicine, and keep us warm.

THINK ABOUT IT

Look at the pictures and think about where plants might be used. Talk about your ideas with a friend.

UNUSUAL PLANTS

Q. What plant has the biggest flower?

A. The rafflesia plant has the largest flower in the world. A rafflesia flower can be up to 3 feet (1 m) wide. However, its flowers smell like rotting animals. Its bad smell attracts insects, which pollinate the plant.

Carnivorous plants catch and eat small animals and insects. They need extra food because they cannot get enough nutrients from the soil in their habitat.

The pitcher plant makes a sweet liquid that attracts insects. The insects fall into the deep pitcher and are eaten by the plant.

When a Venus flytrap feels that an animal has landed on its leaves, its leaves snap shut and trap the animal.

FIND OUT

Find out how other carnivorous plants catch their food.

QUIZ

1. Plant leaves grow underground. True or not true?

a) true
b) not true

2. Which part of a plant makes food?

a) leaves
b) stem
c) flower

3. How do flowers attract insects?

a) by making noises
b) with bright colors
c) by moving toward them

4. Seeds need to be spread around to give plants room to grow. True or not true?

a) true
b) not true

5. Plants do not need sunlight to survive. True or not true?

a) true
b) not true

6. Which type of plant eats small insects?

a) bamboo
b) pitcher plant
c) poppy

Quiz answers

1. b – not true
2. a – leaves
3. b – with bright colors
4. a – true
5. b – not true
6. b – pitcher plant

GLOSSARY

algae a plant with no stem or leaves that lives in or near water

attract to make something want to come toward something else

carbon dioxide a gas that animals breathe out and plants use to make food

carnivorous describes something that eats meat

crop a plant that is grown in large amounts by farmers

damp slightly wet

flowering describes a plant that has flowers

gas something that has the form of air

habitat the area where a plant or an animal lives

herbivore an animal that only eats plants

liquid something that has the form of water and can be poured

microscope a machine that makes small objects look much bigger

nectar a sweet liquid made by plants

nutrient a substance that plants need to get from the soil in order to grow

omnivore an animal that eats plants and other animals

orchard lots of fruit trees grown together

oxygen a gas in the air that animals need to breathe to live

pollen a powder made by flowers, which makes other flowers produce seeds

pollinated when a flower is pollinated, it has received pollen from another flower

reproduce to produce new plants

rotting describes something which is decaying and often smells bad

scatter to throw objects across an area so that they all land in different places

shady describes somewhere that doesn't get much light from the Sun

shoot a new stem or branch of a plant

source where something comes from

INDEX

SOME ANSWERS

p. 6–7 1.A; 2.C; 3.D; 4.B.
p. 8–9 A roots; B stem; C leaf.
p. 11 Most seeds lie in the soil and wait for warmer weather to return in the spring.
p. 13 Ellie's seed needs soil or compost, and water. It will also need to be placed in a sunny spot.
p. 15 Spring.
p. 19 Animals can spread seeds in their droppings.
p. 20–21 Bottom row on the right. Its leaves have wilted.
p. 22–23 1.B; 2.D; 3.C; 4.A.
p. 24–25 A. roots; B. leaves; C. seeds; D. fruit; E. stem and tender leaves; F. flower.